Hanover Ontario in Colour Photos, Saving Our History One Photo at a Time

Photography
by Barbara Raué
2013

Series Name:
Cruising Ontario

Book 57: Hanover

Cover photo: Gothic Cottage

Series Name: Cruising Ontario
Saving Our History One Photo at a Time

Photos now in full colour
Check the Appendixes in the back of each book for
descriptions of architectural terms and building styles

Other Books by Barbara Raue

Coins of Gold

Arrows, Indians and Love

The Life and Times of Barbara
Volume 1: Inventions That Have Enhanced My Life
Volume 2: Entertainment That I Have Enjoyed
Volume 3: East Coast Trips
Volume 4: Olympics Have Always Intrigued Me
Volume 5: Wonders of the World
Volume 6: Caribbean Cruises We Have Enjoyed
Volume 7: Animals
Volume 8: Storms and Other Major Disasters in My Lifetime
Volume 9: Wars, Terrorist Attacks and Major Disasters

The Cromwell Family Book

Visit Barbara's website to view all of her books
http://barbararaue.ericraue.com

Hanover

In 1849, the first pioneer, Abraham Buck, stood on the banks of the Saugeen River and looked about him at the thick forest of hardwood timber where the deer, bear and wolf ran free. The sky was filled with wild pigeons and the streams teamed with fish. He expressed the words, "It is good for us to be here."

Mr. Buck was joined by others, such as: Christian Hassenjager, the first of many German settlers; Abram Gottwals, a missionary with the Evangelical Church; Duncan Campbell, the first postmaster; Edward Goodeve opened one of the first stores; entrepreneurs such as Henry Proctor Adams who built the dam and the first mill and drew up plans for the village – a man of vision who could foresee the future growth of the town; Dr. Landerkin, the first doctor; and Daniel Knechtel, an eager, hard-working man who arrived in 1864 with a bag of tools on his back and began making furniture in a small barn behind his house. His vision and determination guided Hanover for more than a century. Hanover is located on Grey/Bruce County Road 4, east of Walkerton and west of Durham. Hanover marks the boundary between Grey County and Bruce County.

Led by men such as Daniel Knechtel, Henry Peppler and Jared Spiesz, the village grew and prospered with large factories and new businesses manufacturing furniture, knitted goods, cement, milled products and other items. Roads were improved, street lighting was added, and facilities for education and recreation were built.

The coming of the railway enabled the factories to ship their goods from coast to coast and by the 1920s, the town was known for its fine furniture and given the title of "The Furniture Capital of Canada". During the depression, the large furniture factories and other associated plants kept on working with a reduced work force.

Hanover moved forward into the 1950s with factories continuing to manufacture fine, hardwood furniture, textiles, flour, processed food and kitchen cabinets.

The milk wagons were pulled by horses plodding from door to door along the shady streets, but this ended as larger grocery stores with refrigeration opened. New schools and additions were needed to meet the expanding numbers of children; the population of one school in 1959 included twelve sets of twins and two sets of triplets.

The decades from 1970 to the year 2000 saw the decline of manufacturing, especially in the large factory settings. The older factories producing hardwood furniture could not compete with the cheaper, imported products. Railway freight began to decrease as highways improved and transport trucking took over.

Smaller businesses replaced the giant factory complexes. The unused rail lines are now scenic walking trails. The old Knechtel factory on the main street has been replaced by Heritage Square. The Carnegie library was expanded to include the Civic Centre, Town Hall and refurbished Library quarters. A new clock tower houses the old post office clock works.

(Information gathered from History on the Hanover website)

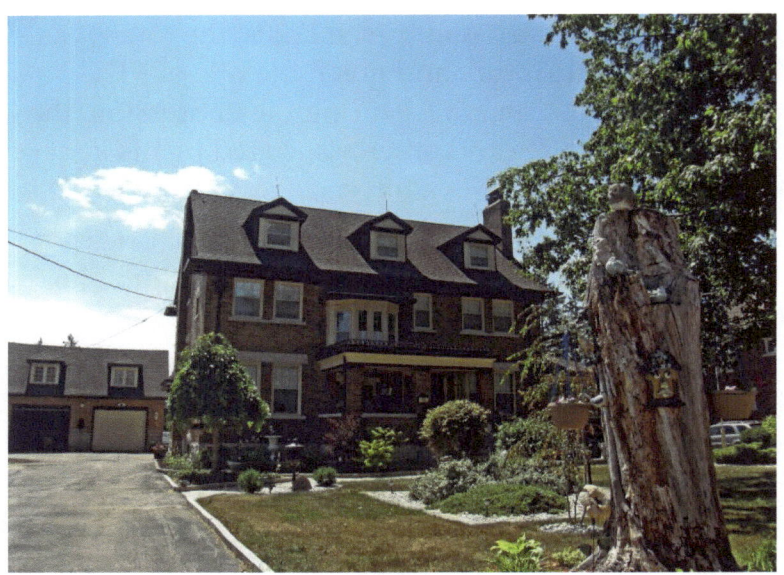

#75 – dormers in the attic

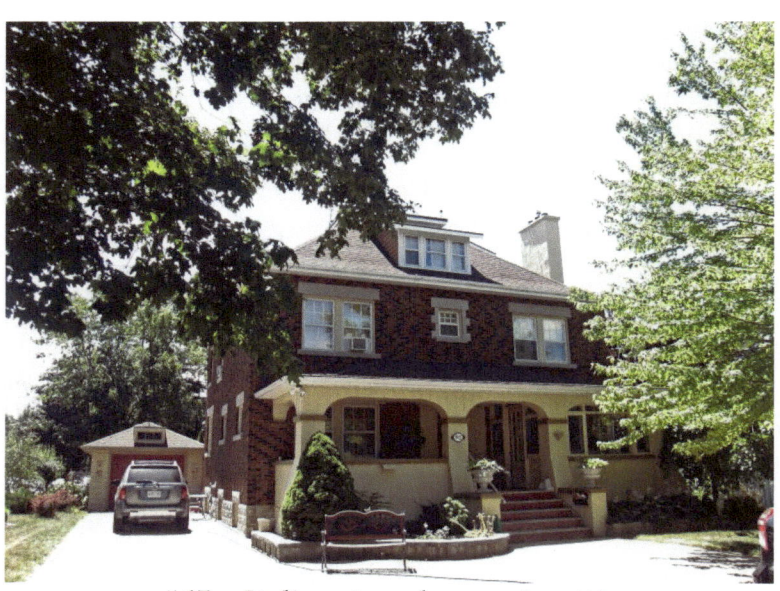

#65 – Italianate – dormer in attic

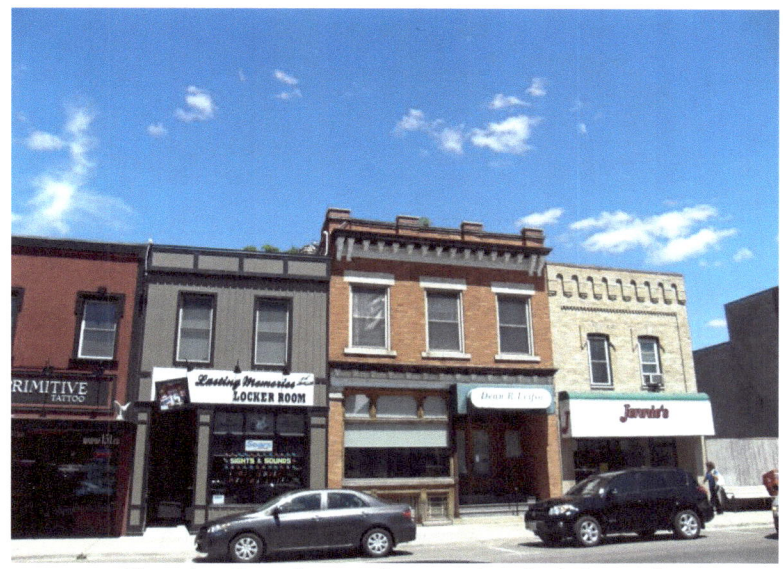

Cornice brackets, decorative brickwork

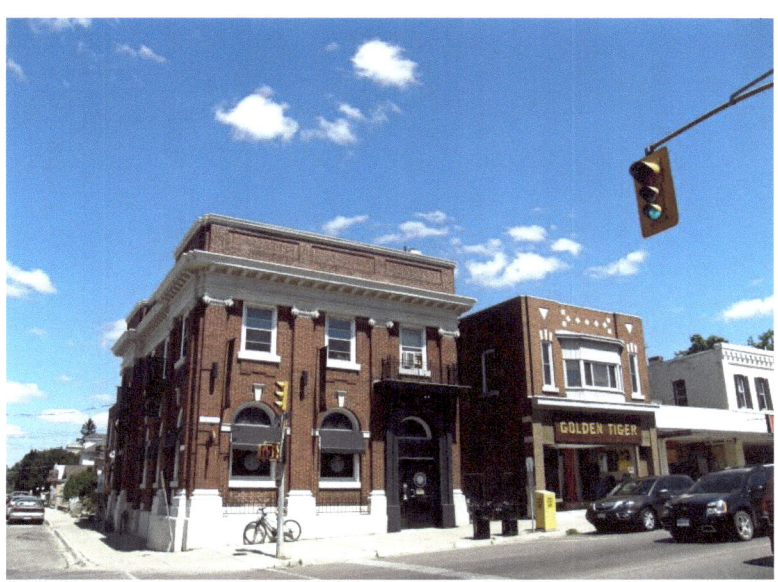

Pilasters with scrollwork capitals

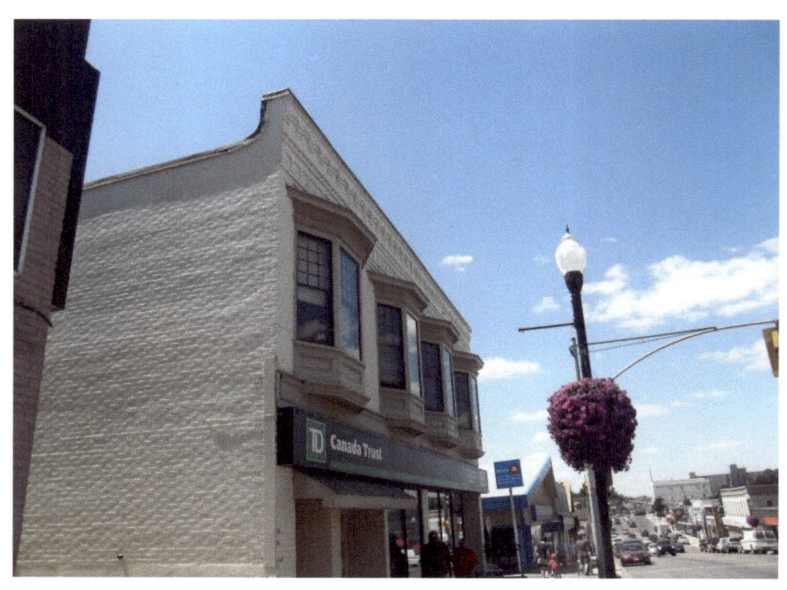

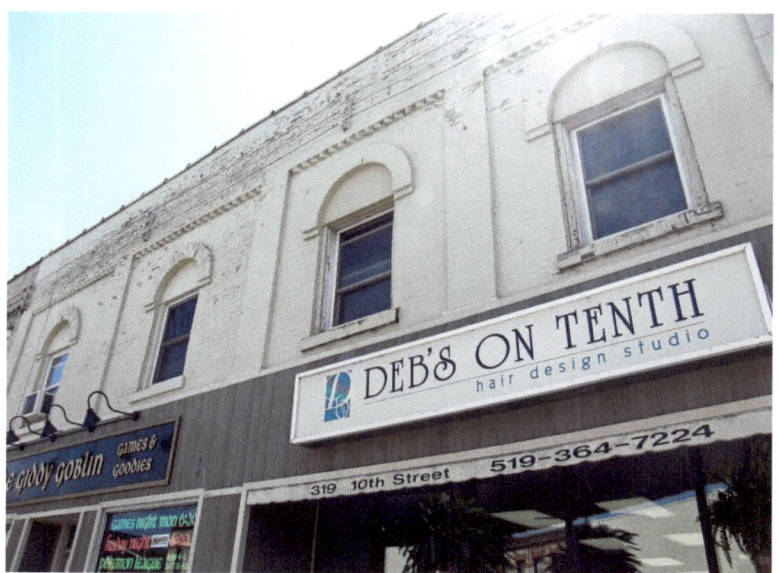

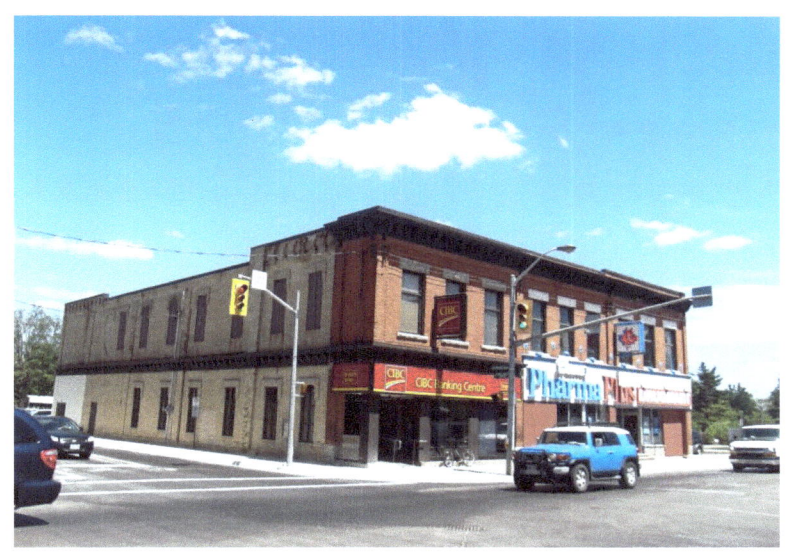

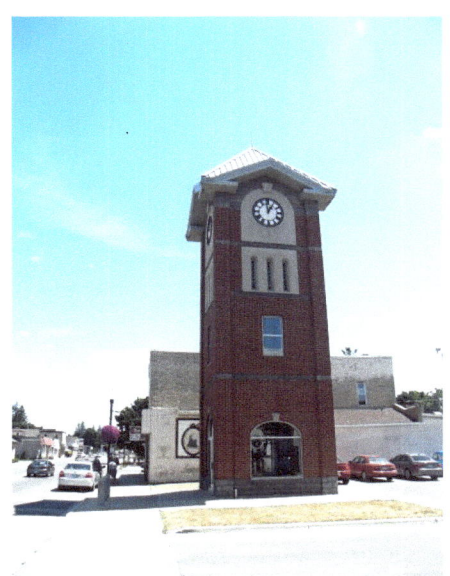

Clock Tower with original clock from the Old Post Office

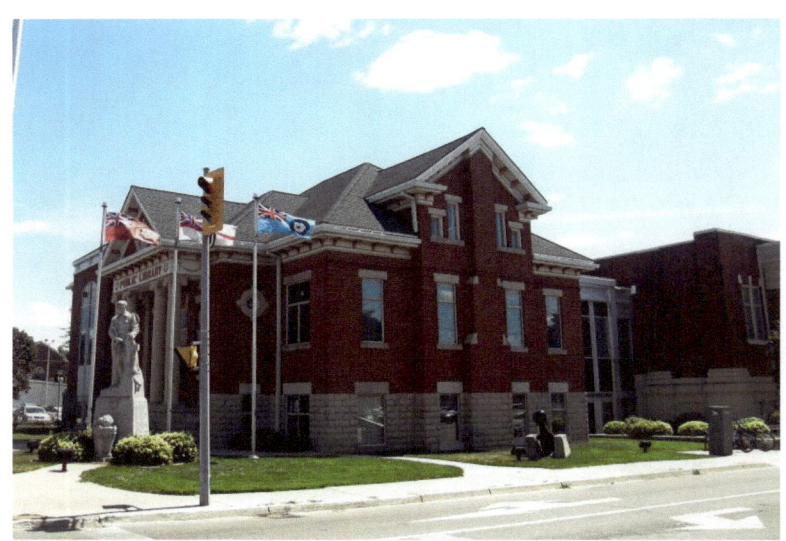

Public Library in Beaux Arts style – pillars with capitals,
pediment with window in tympanum

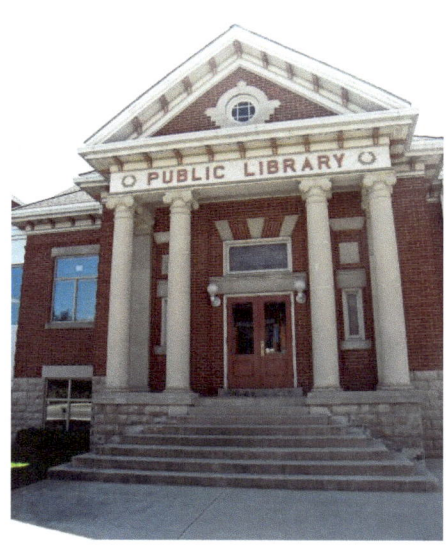

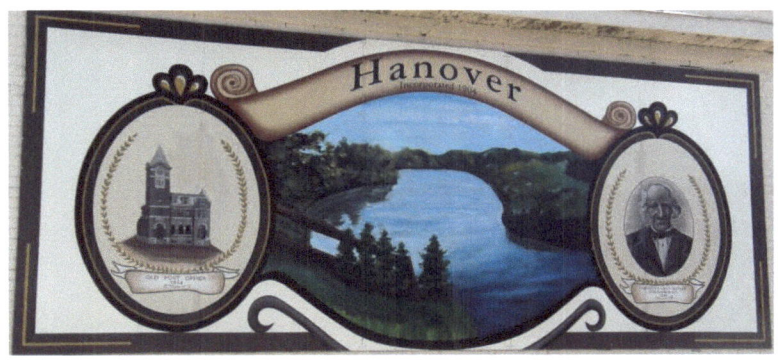

The mural was painted by Cameron Mahy of the Rocky River Sign Company Incorporated and is eight feet high by twenty feet in length.

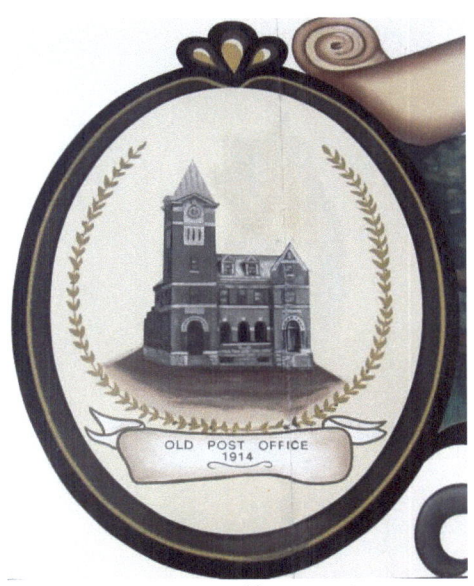

Old Post Office – 1914

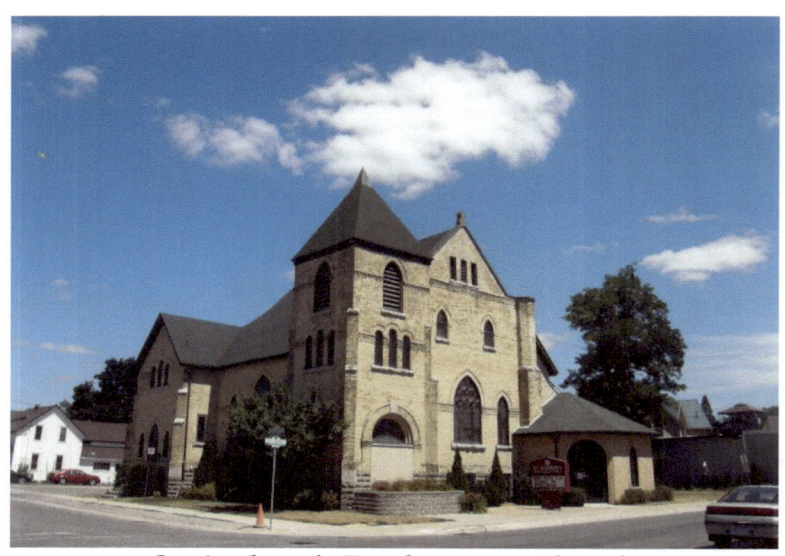

St. Andrew's Presbyterian Church
Corner of 11th Avenue and 10th Street
Lancet windows, dentil moulding, arched window voussoirs
with keystones

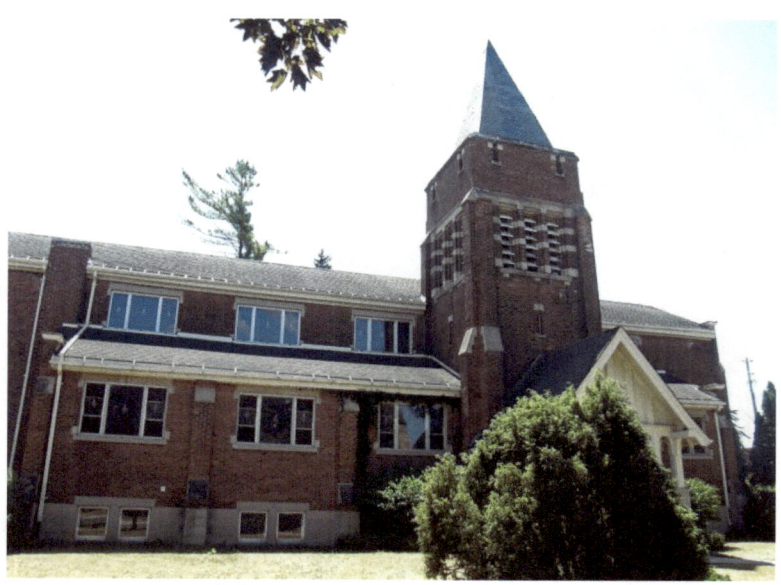

Hanover Baptist Church

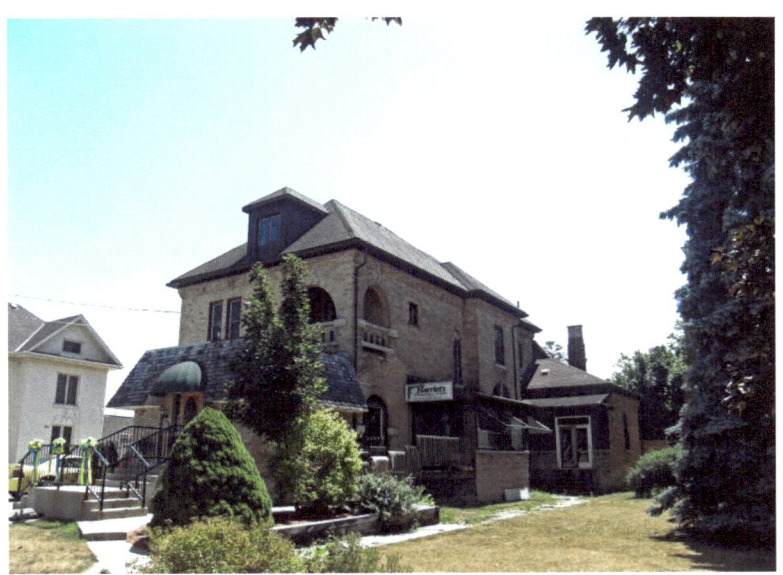

Italianate style, dormer in attic, hipped roof

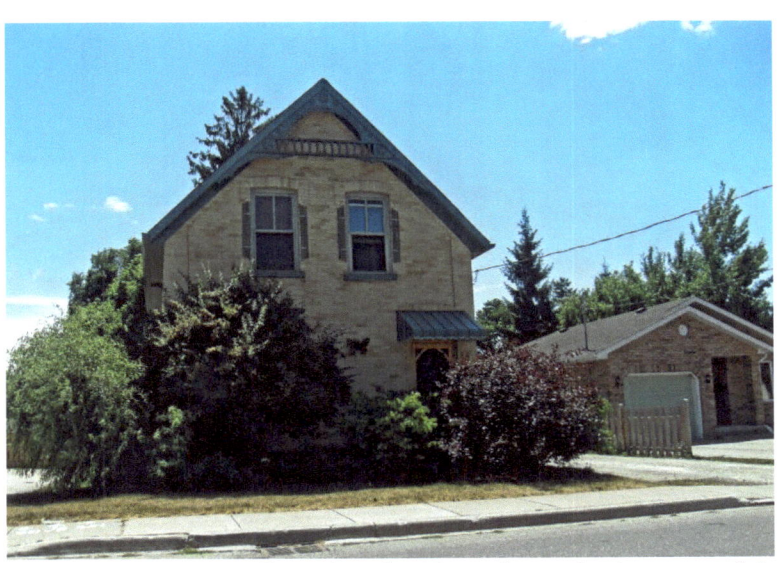

Gothic Revival, yellow brick, Vergeboard trim on gable

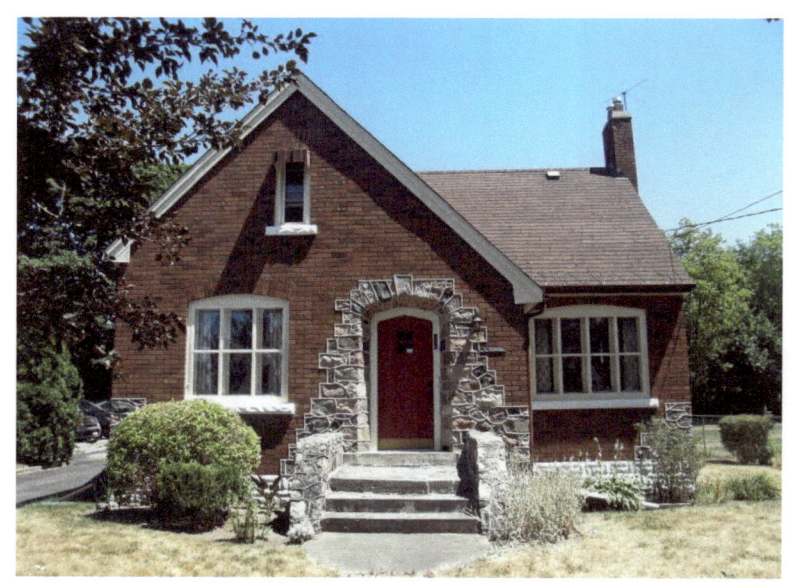

439 13th Avenue – Gothic style

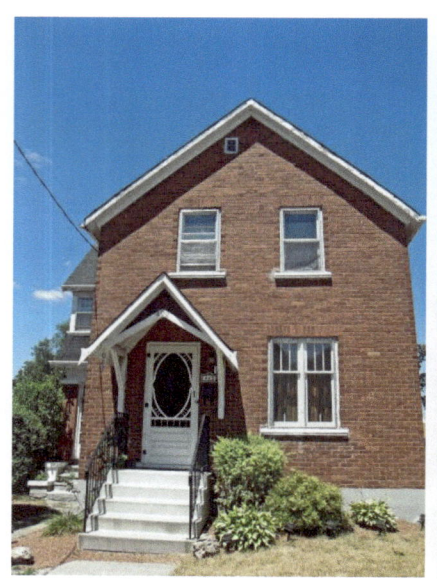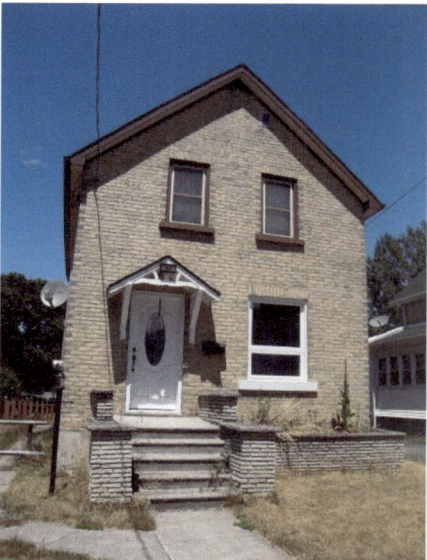

462 13th Avenue

Gothic Revival style

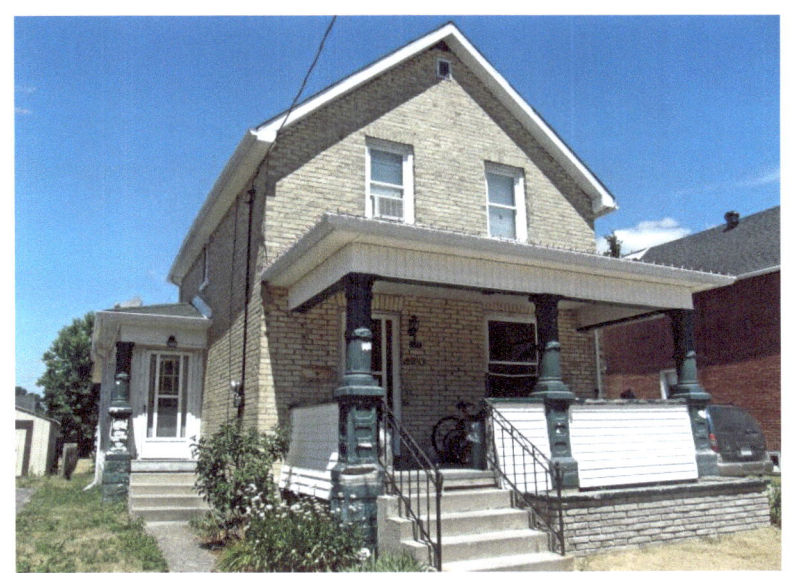

470 13th Avenue – Gothic Revival

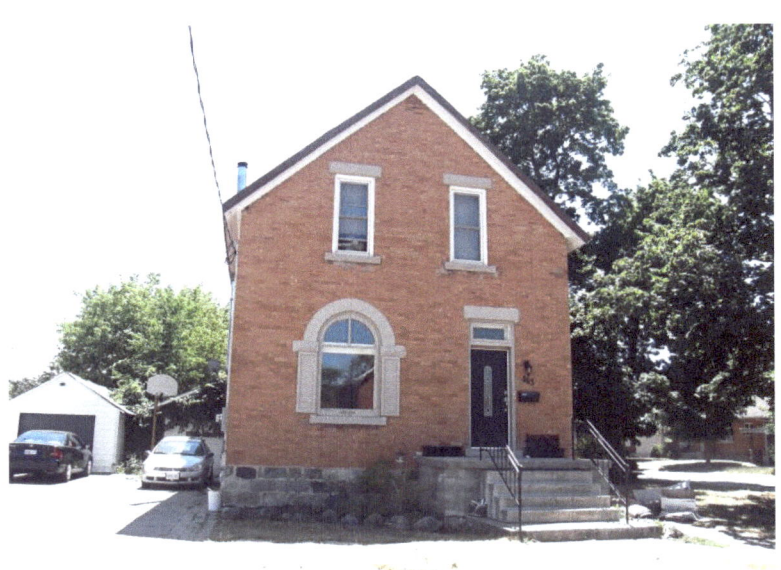

463 13th Avenue – Gothic Revival, cobblestone basement

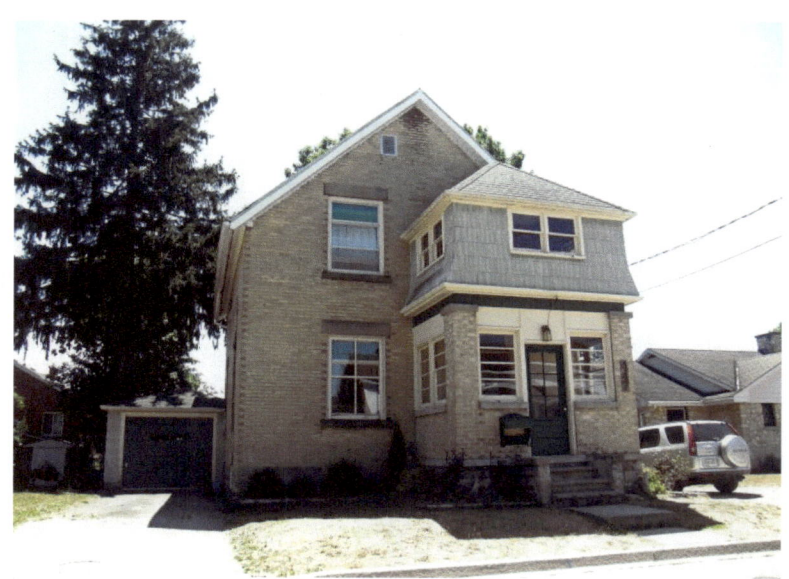

Gothic Revival in yellow brick

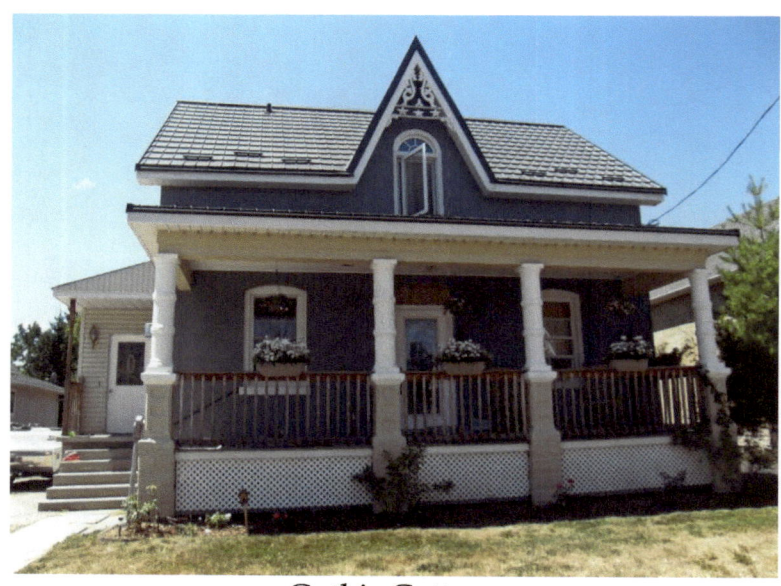

Gothic Cottage

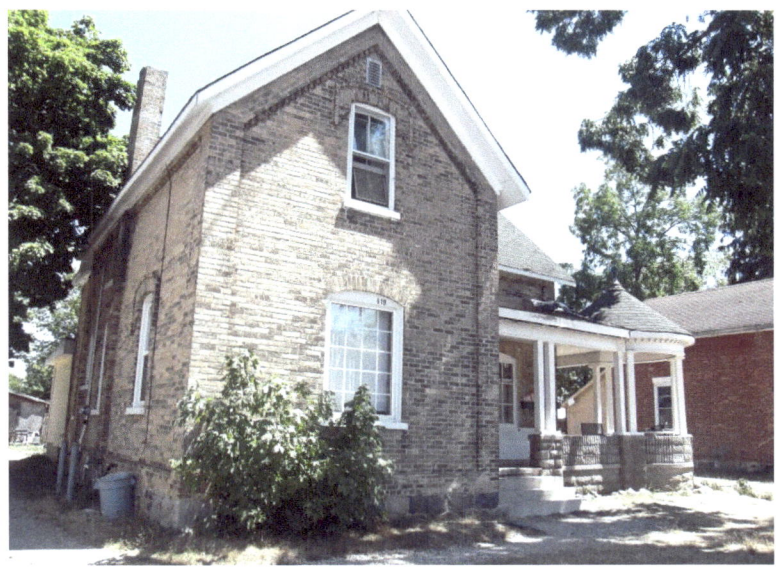

#519

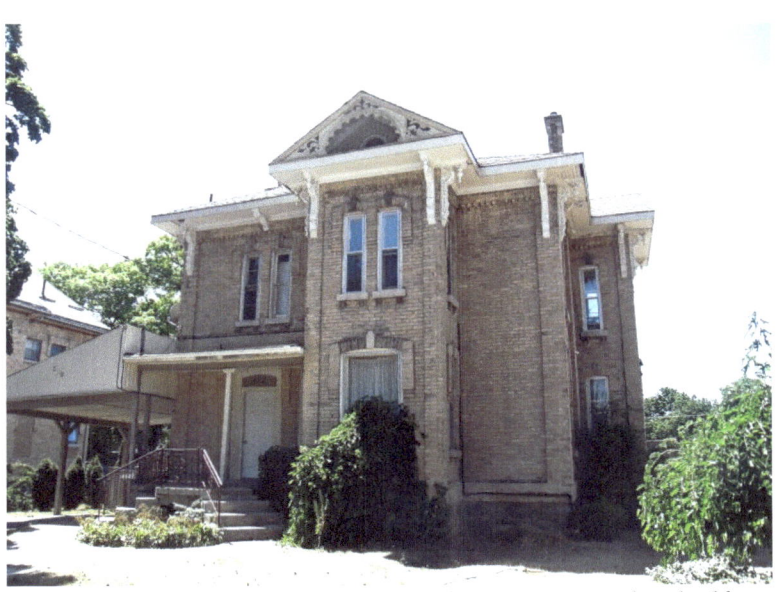

#512 – Italianate style, cornice brackets, two-and-a-half storey
tower-like bay with decorative gable

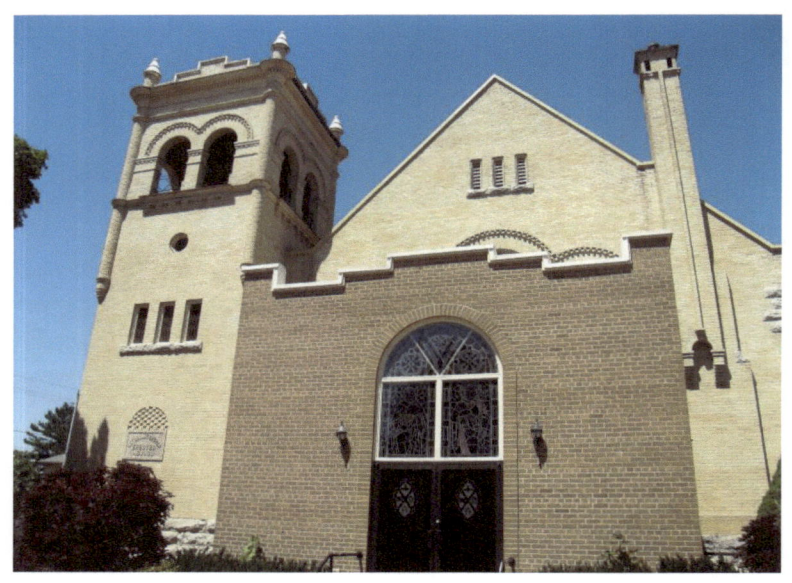

Methodist Church erected 1900
Now Grace United Church

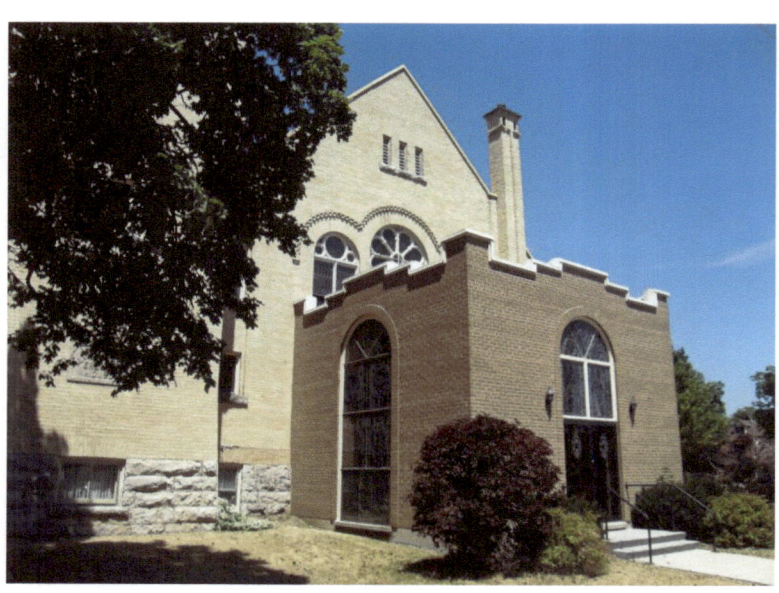

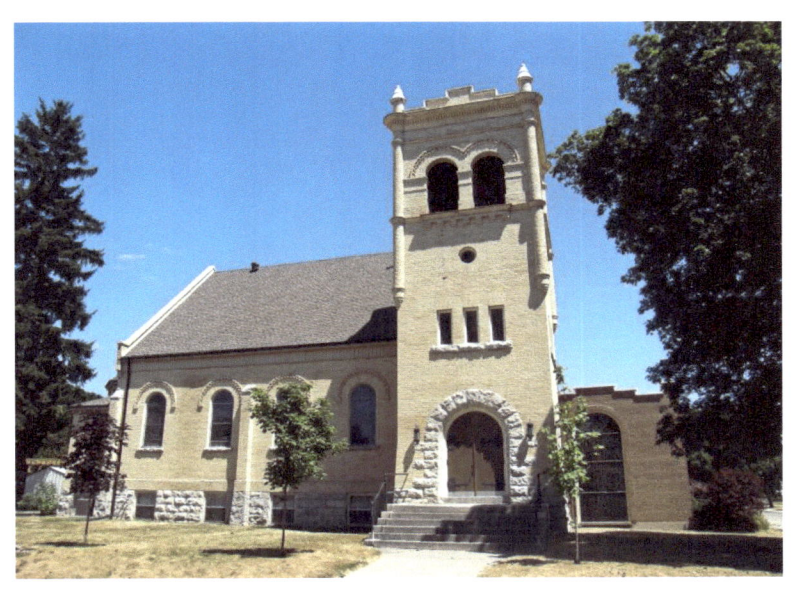

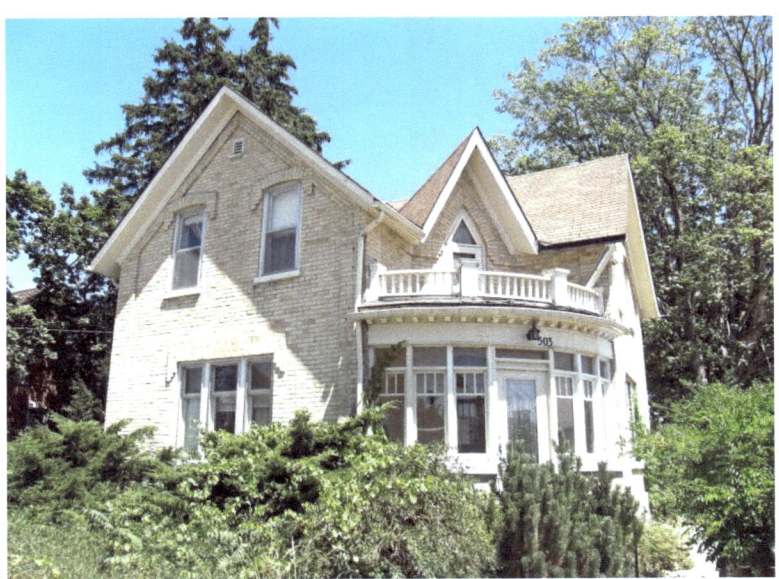

#503 – Gothic Revival

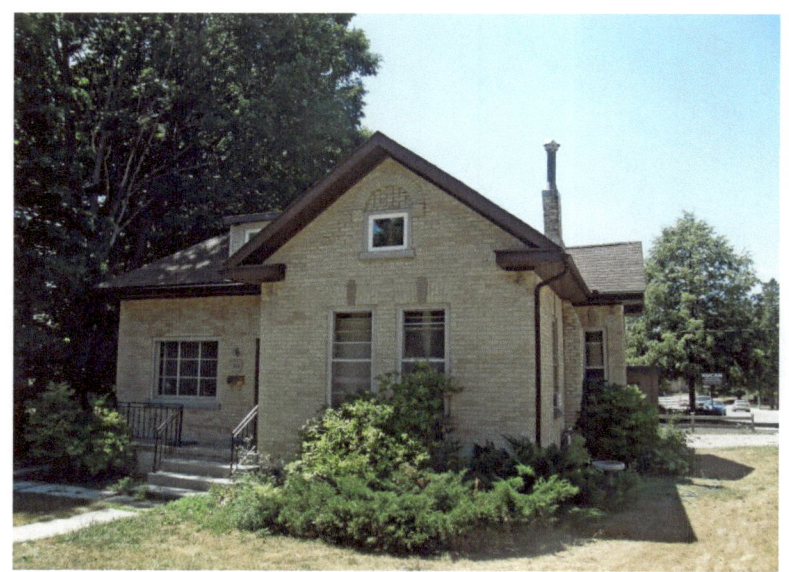

514 9th Avenue

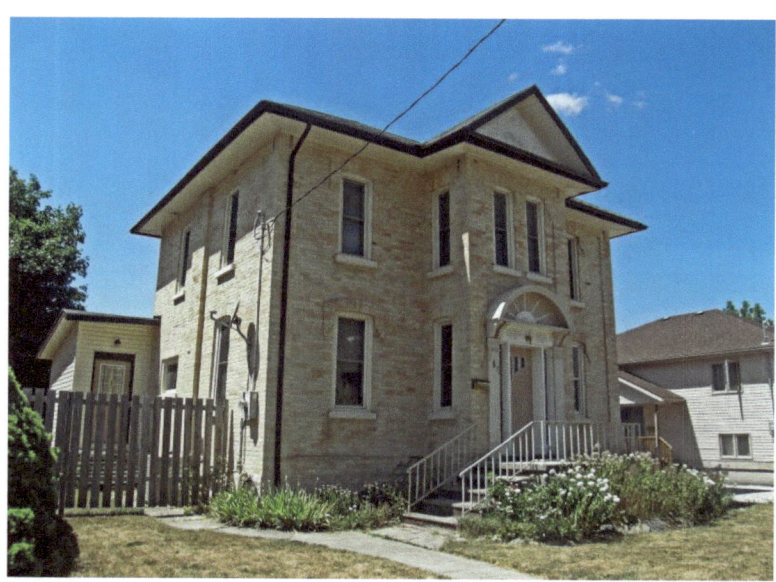

540 9th Avenue – Italianate style with two storey tower-like bay topped with gable

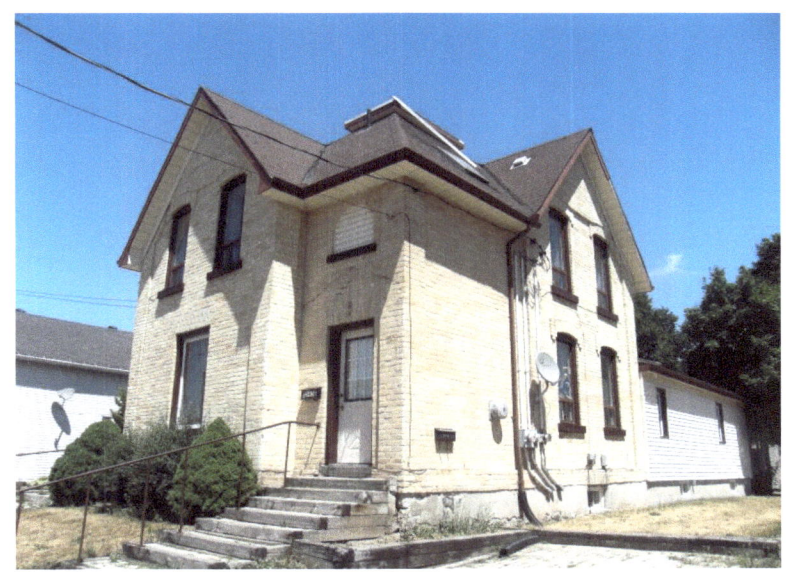

545 9th Avenue – Gothic Revival

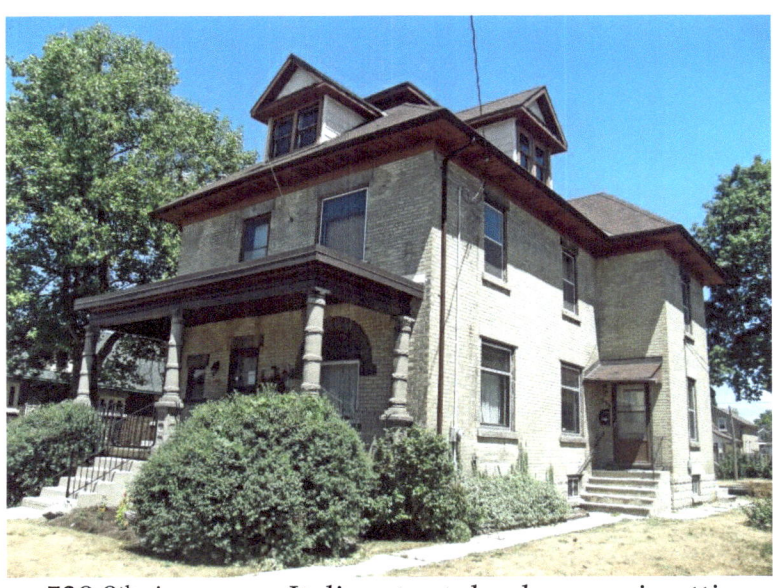

539 9th Avenue – Italianate style, dormers in attic

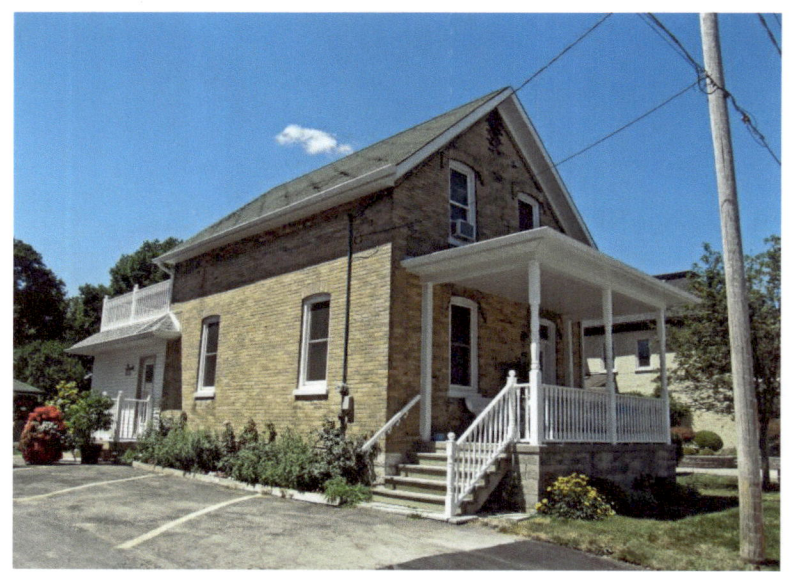

546 9th Avenue – Gothic Revival in yellow brick

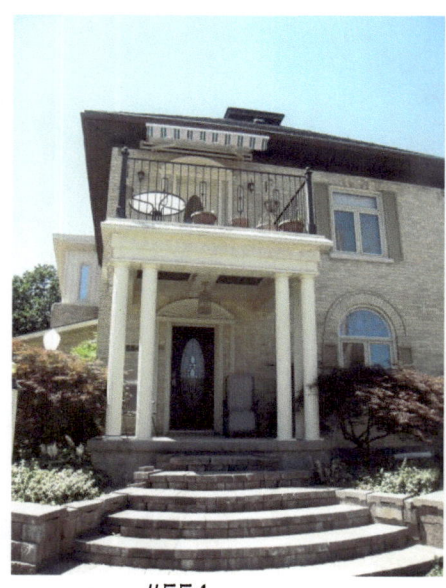

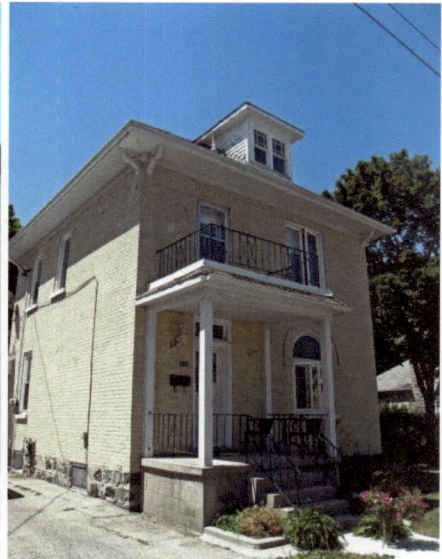

#554

#586 - Italianate

9th Avenue

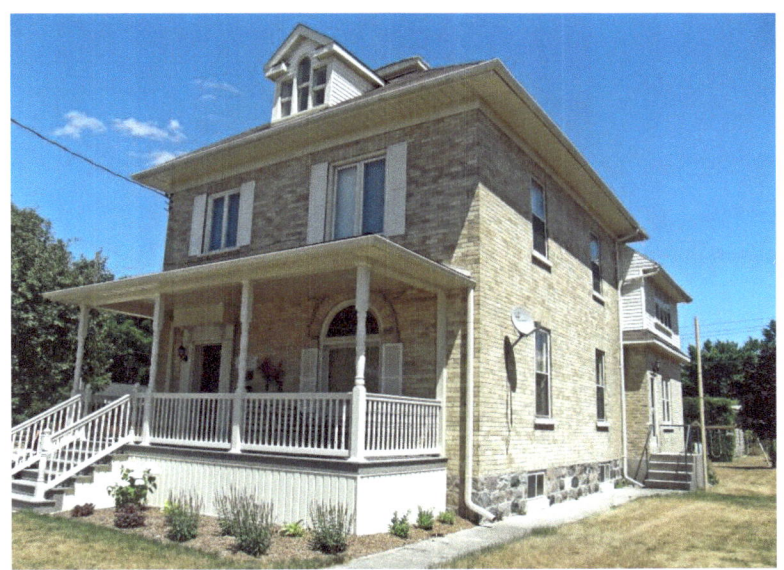

Italianate with dormer in attic

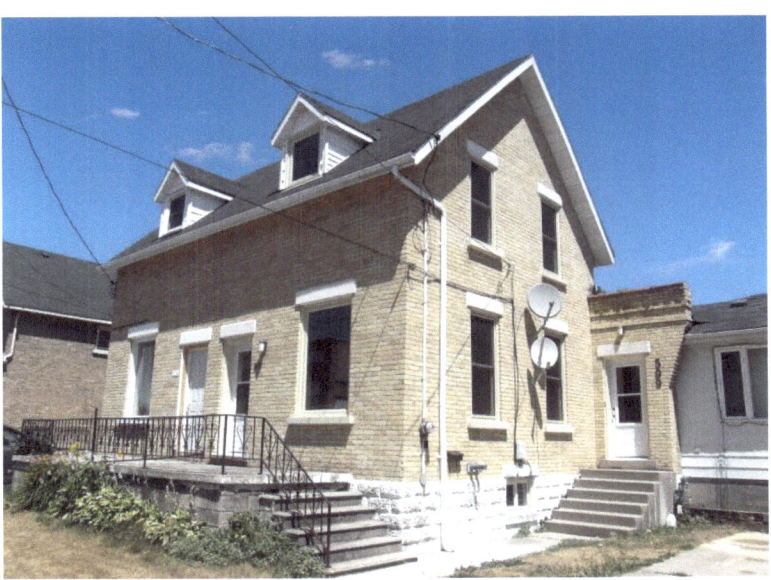

601 9th Avenue – Gothic Revival with dormers in attic

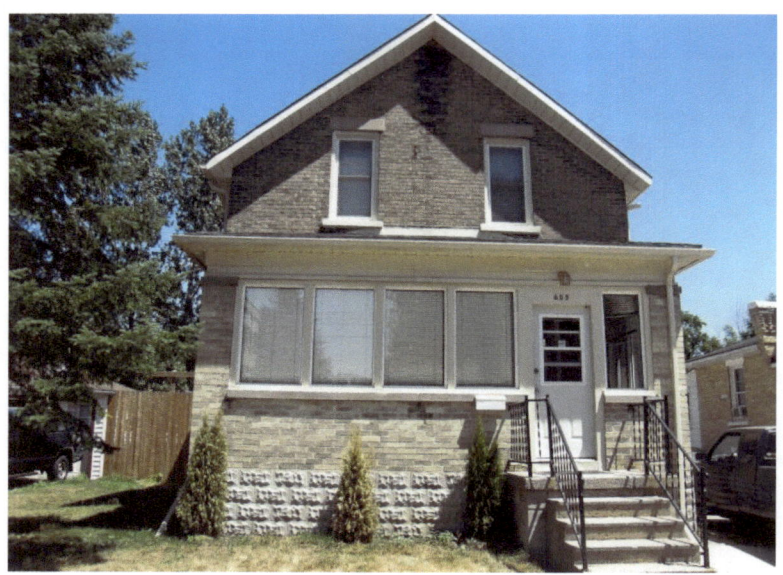

605 9th Avenue

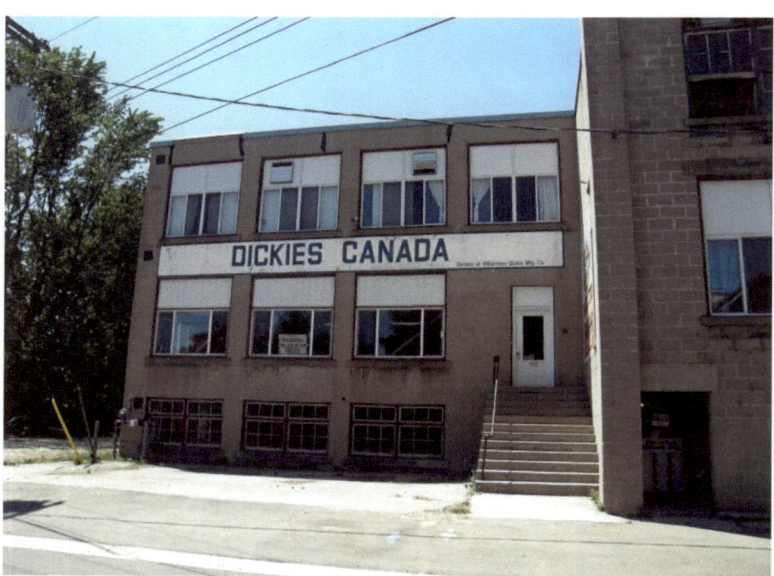

Dickies Canada produced clothing for the work wear industry
with traditional matched sets of work shirts and work pants.
A Hanover outlet store still operates although manufacturing
stopped in December 2009.

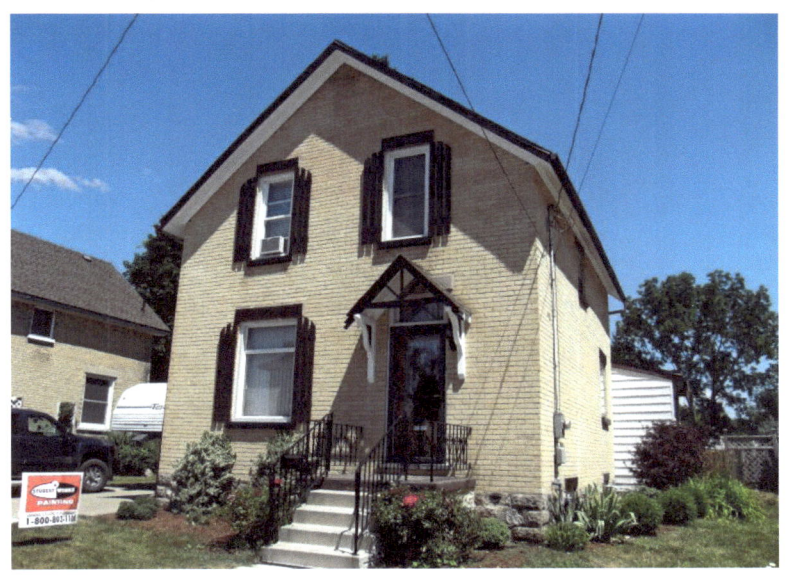

Gothic Revival

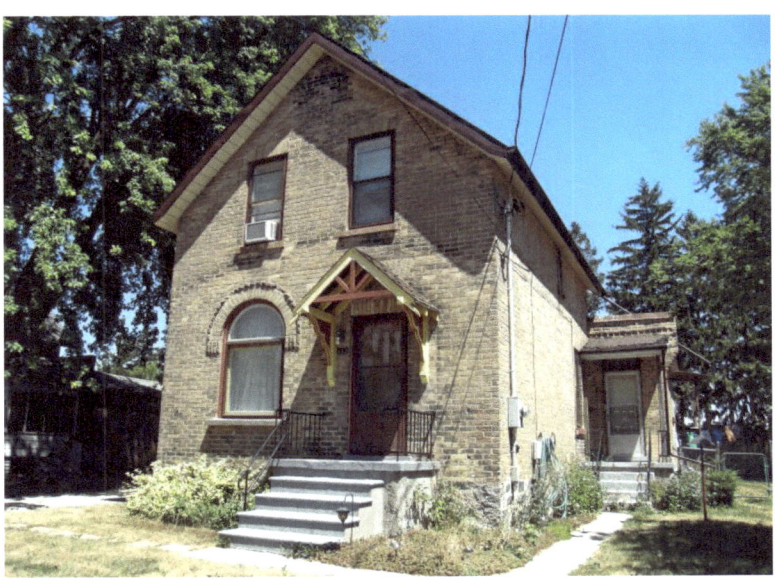

633 9th Avenue – yellow brick, cobblestone basement

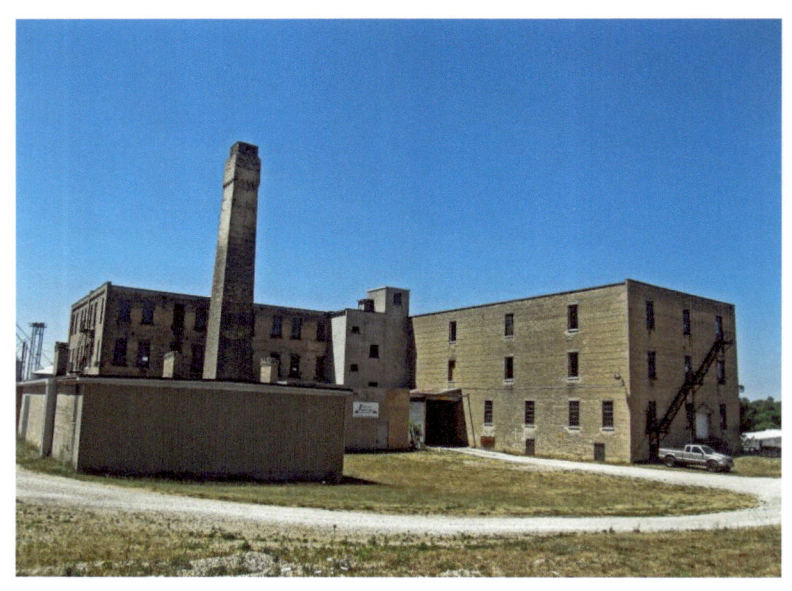

14th Street

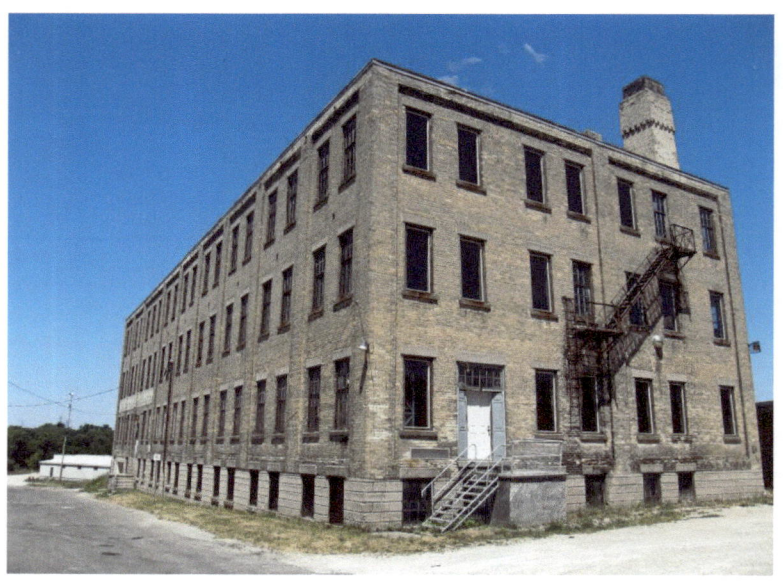

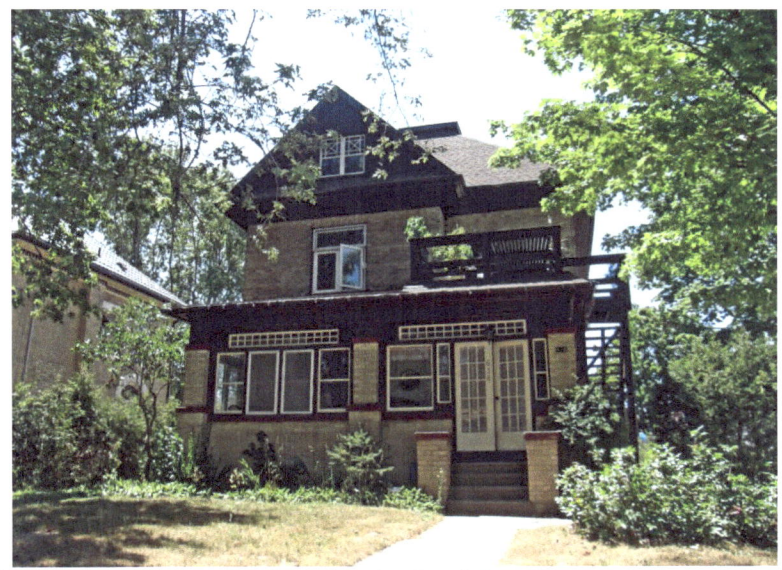

638 9th Avenue – Gothic Revival with newer enclosed porch

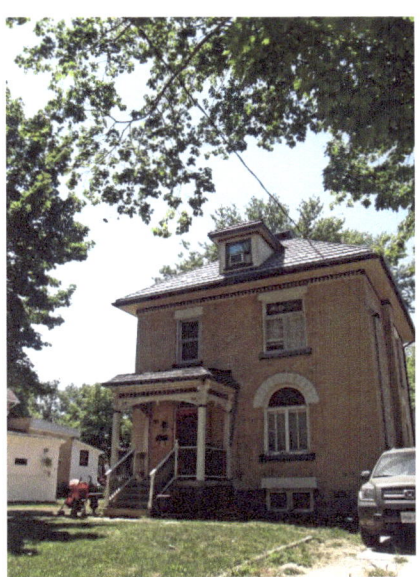

632 9th Avenue
Italianate

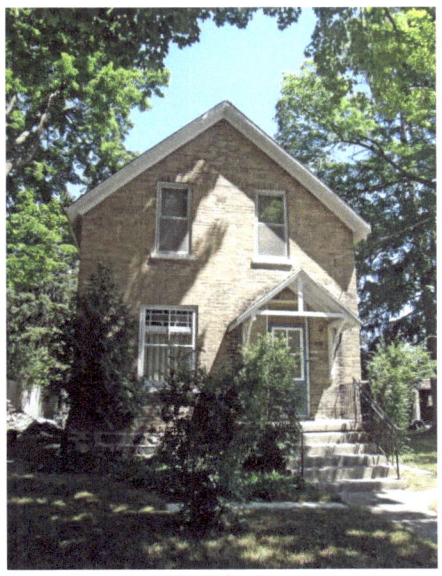

625 9th Avenue
Gothic Revival

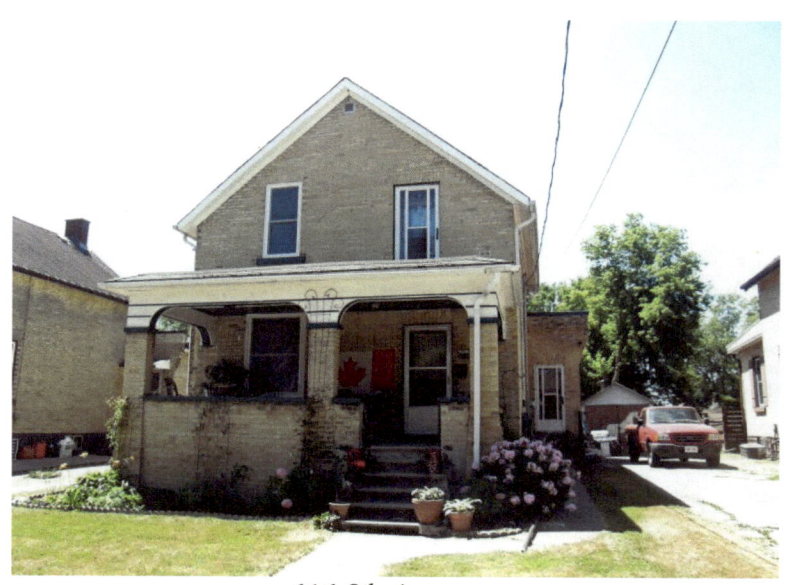

616 9th Avenue

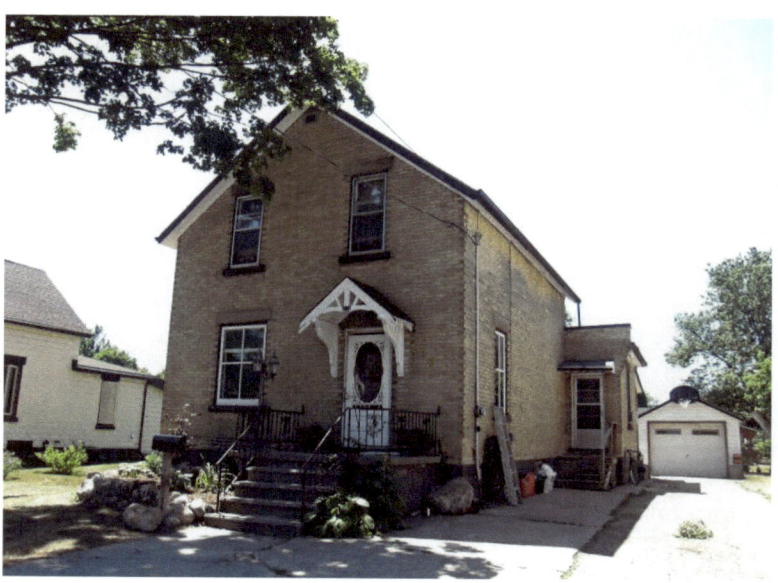

612 9th Avenue

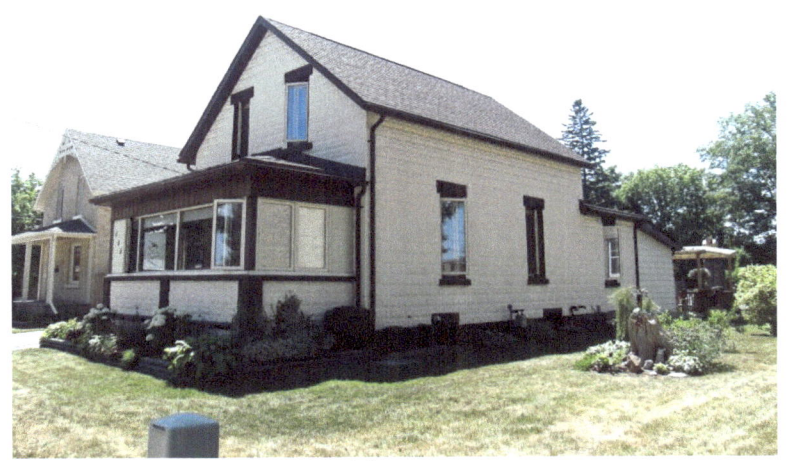

606 9th Avenue

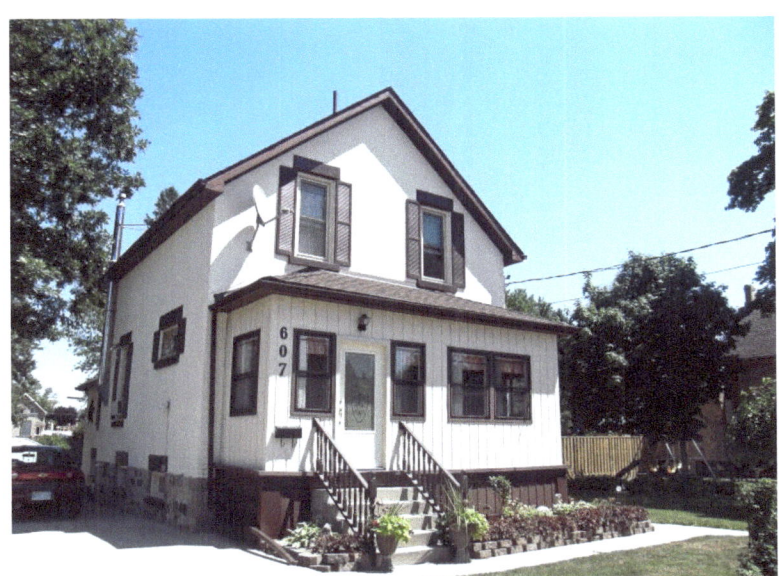

607 9th Avenue – Gothic Revival

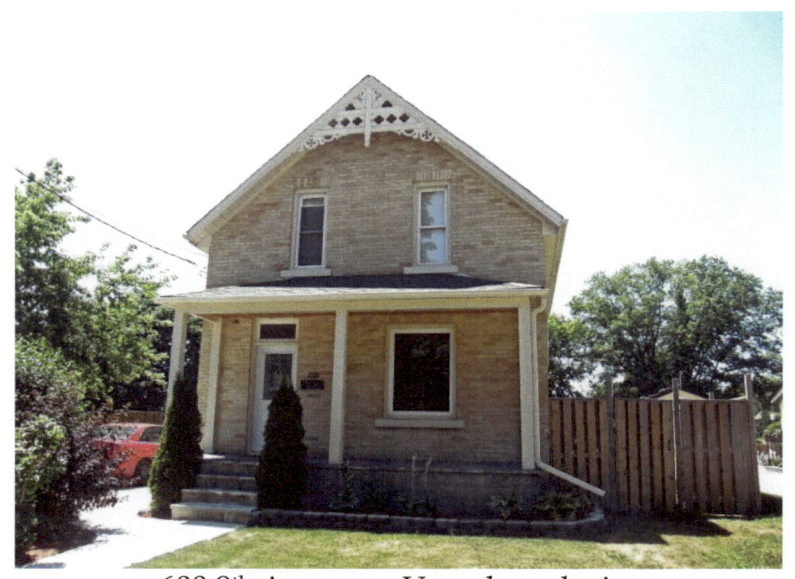

600 9th Avenue – Vergeboard trim

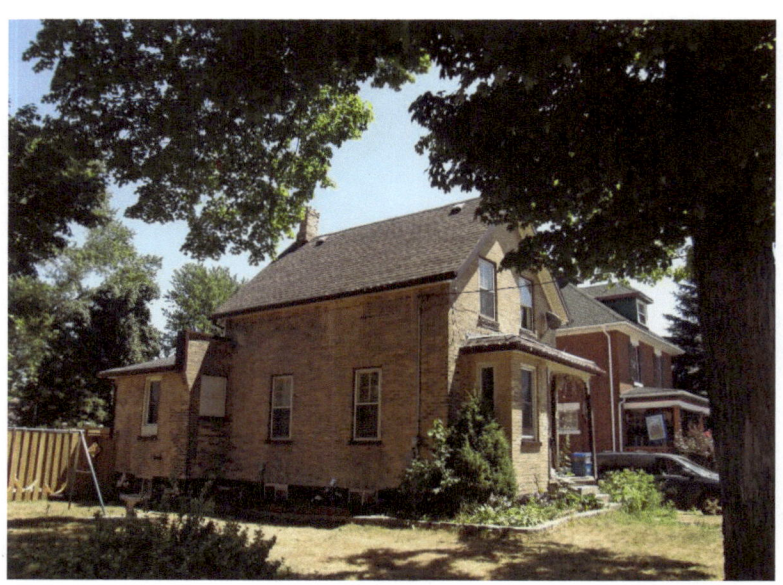

Yellow brick

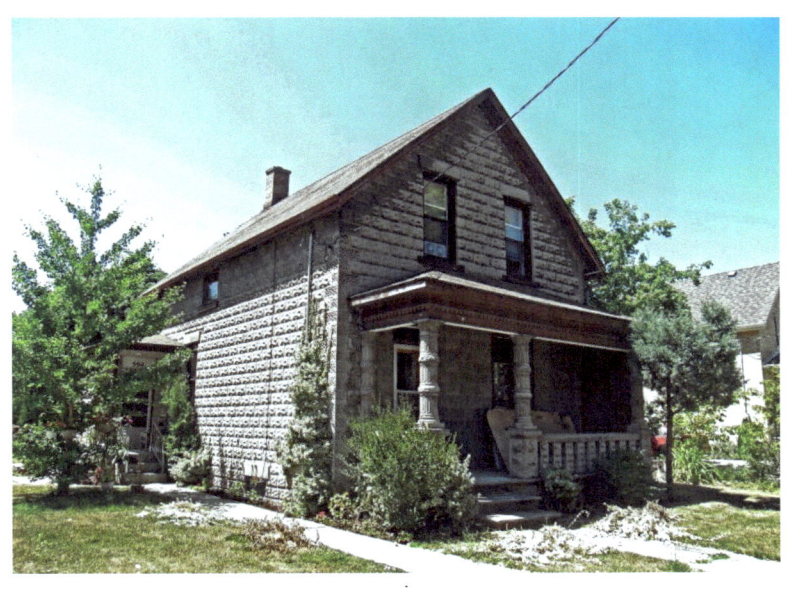

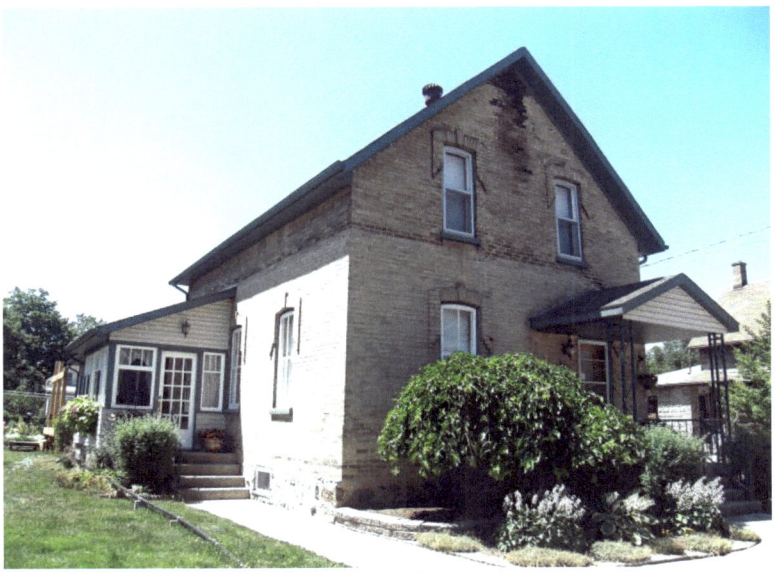

Cobblestone basement

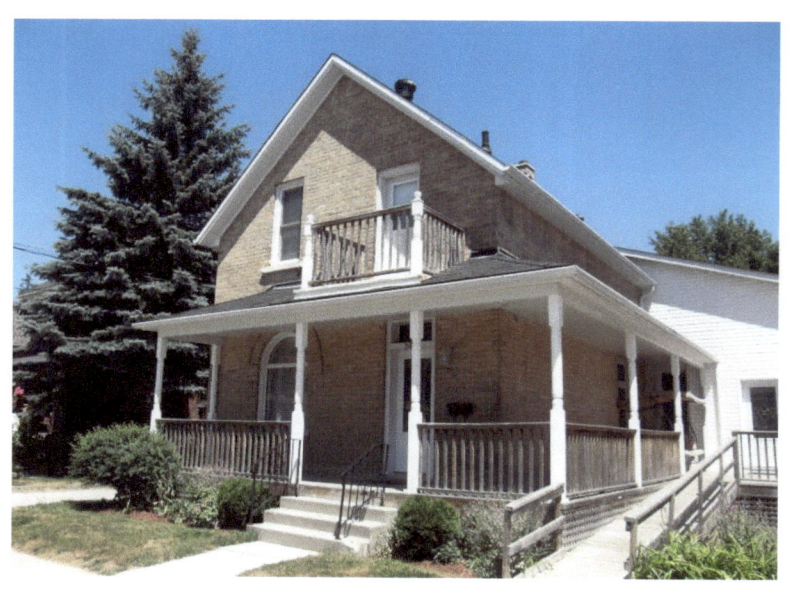

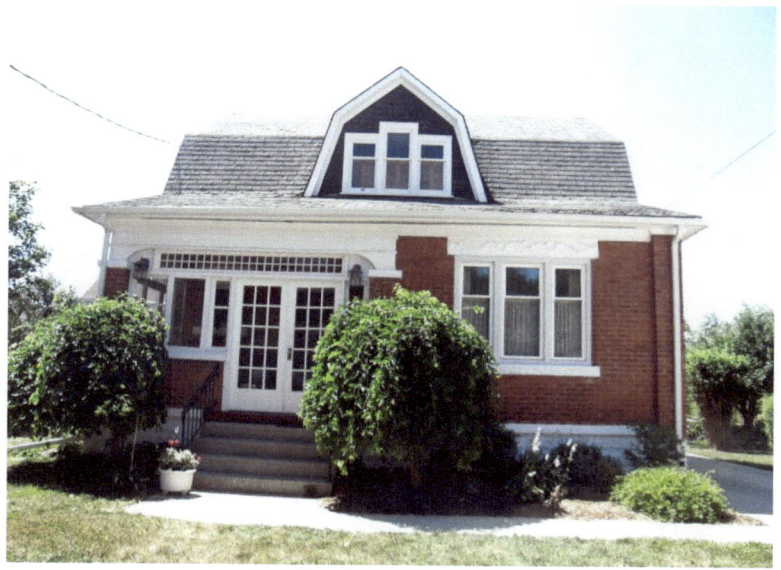

Palladian window

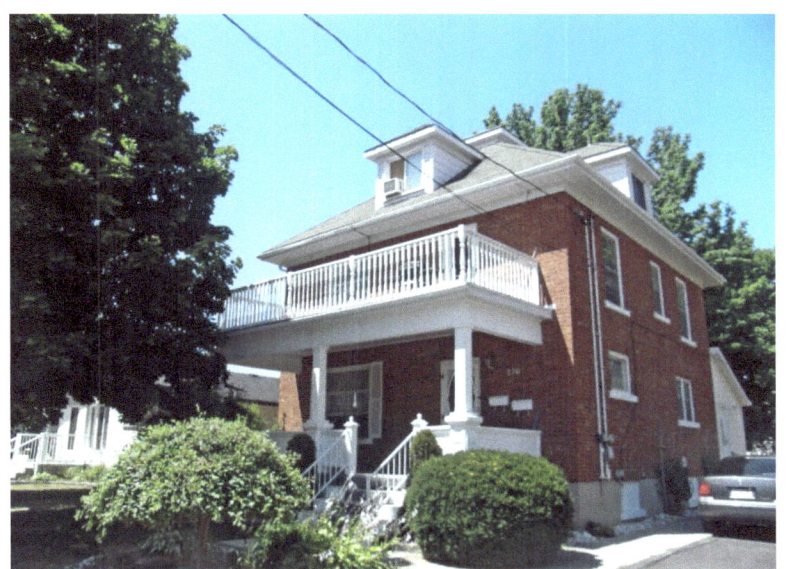

270 8th Avenue – Italianate, dormers in attic, balcony above verandah

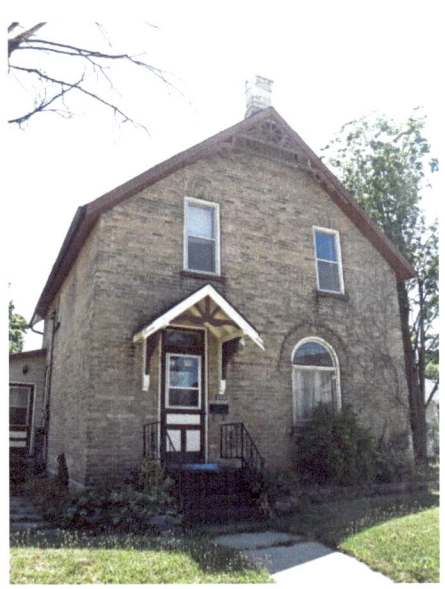

253 8th Avenue

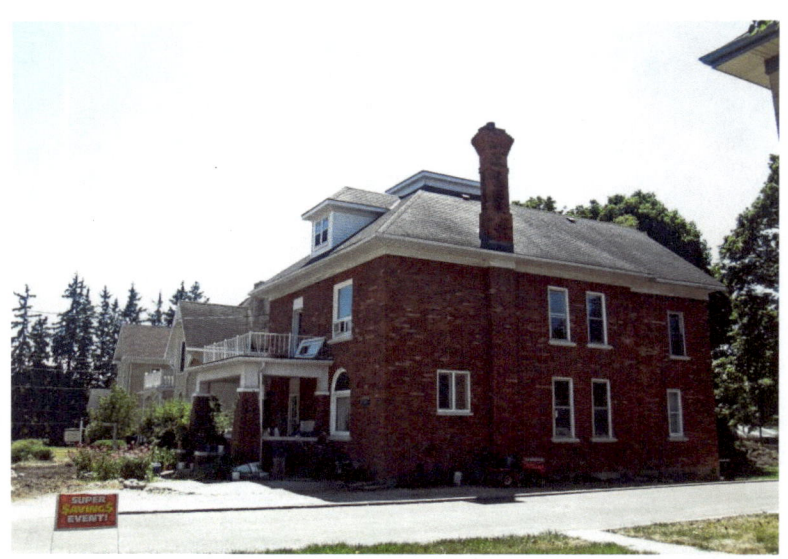

548 8th Avenue - Italianate

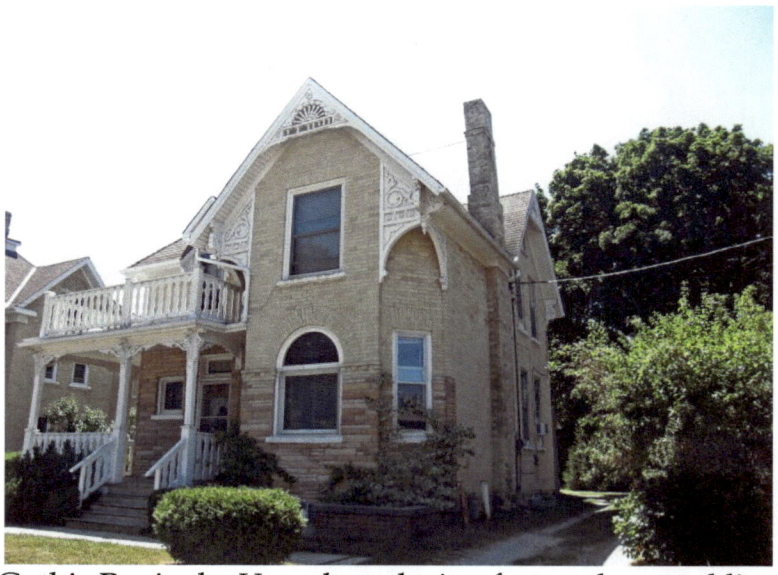

Gothic Revival – Vergeboard trim, fretwork resembling
brackets, yellow brick

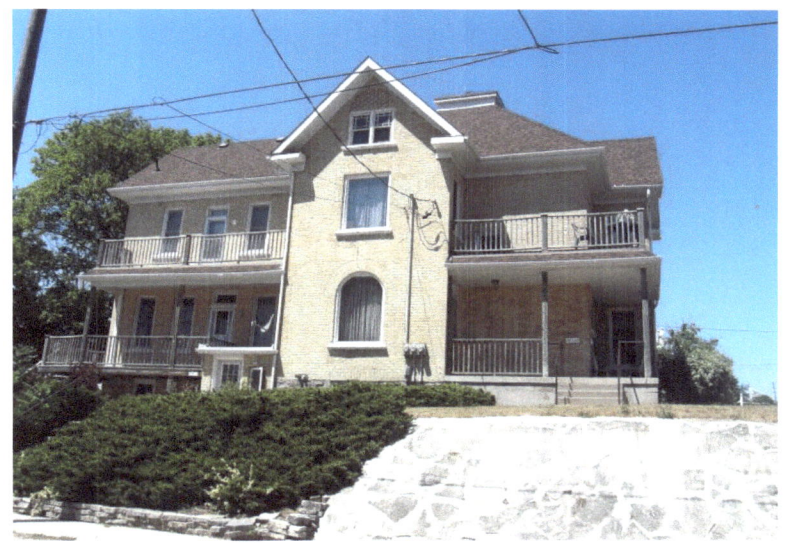

534 12th Street

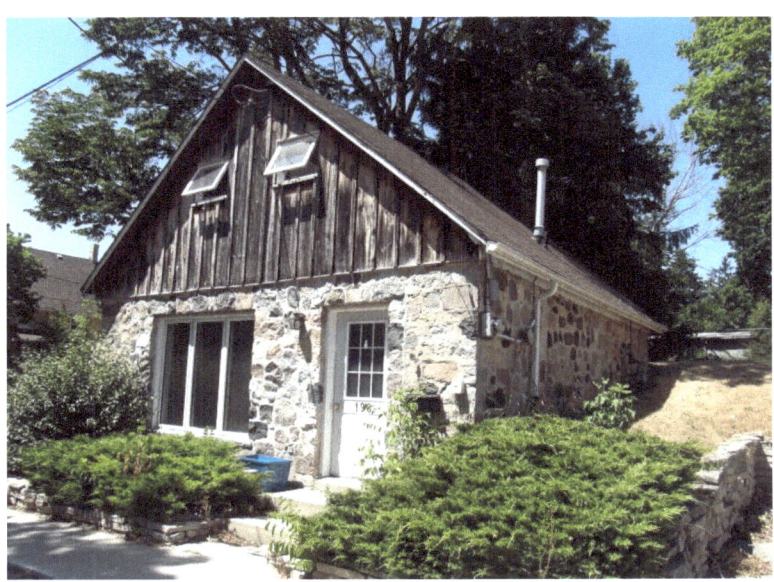

198 12th Street – cobblestone architecture

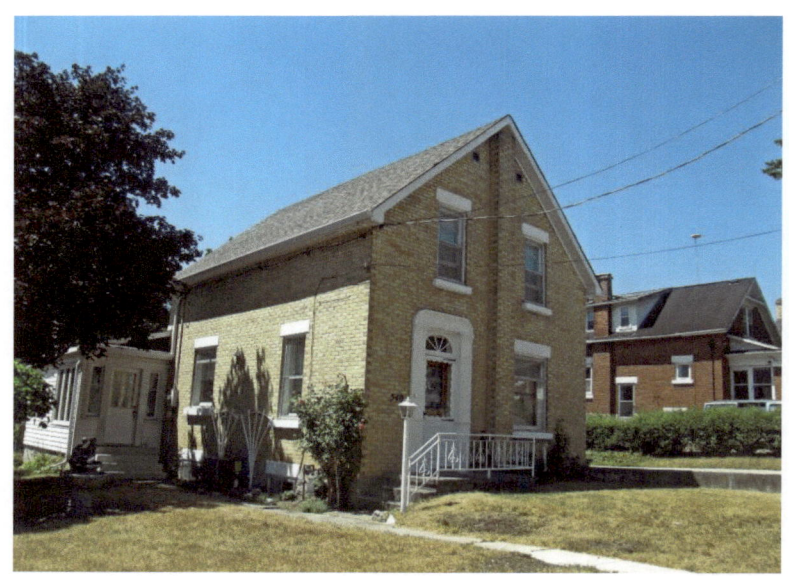

540 12th Street – Gothic Revival – yellow brick

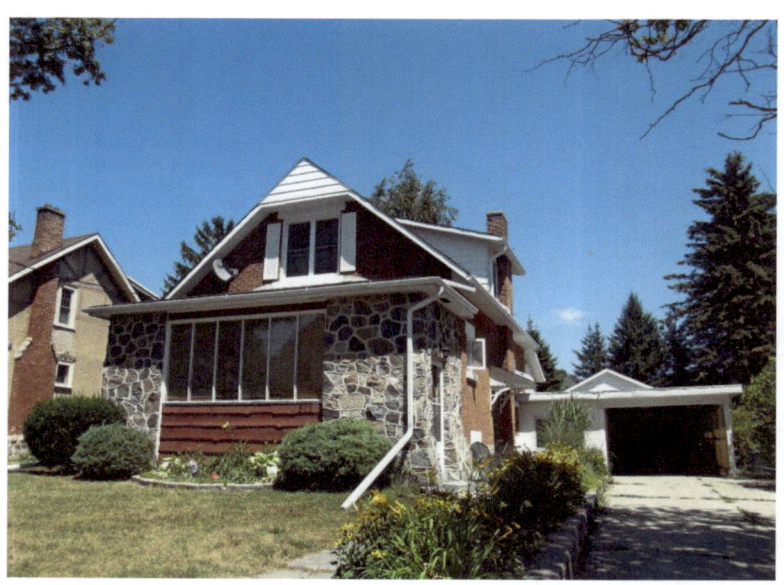

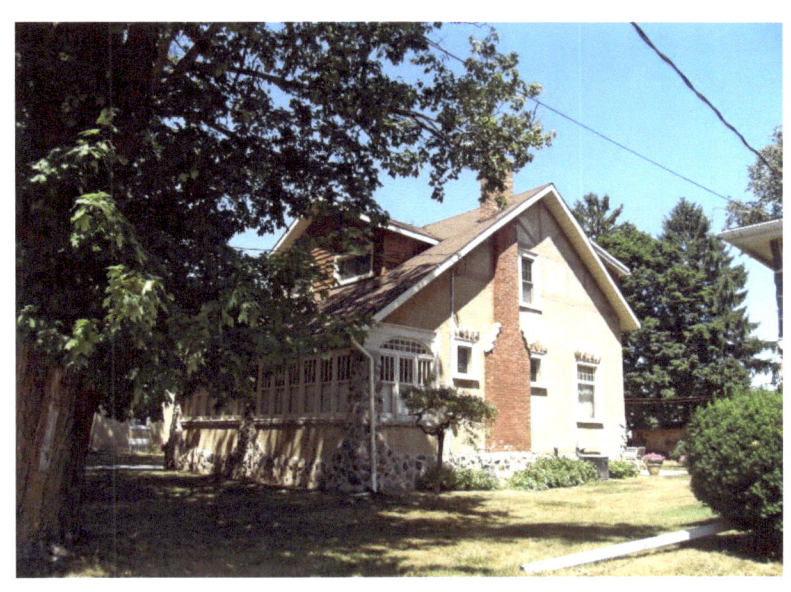

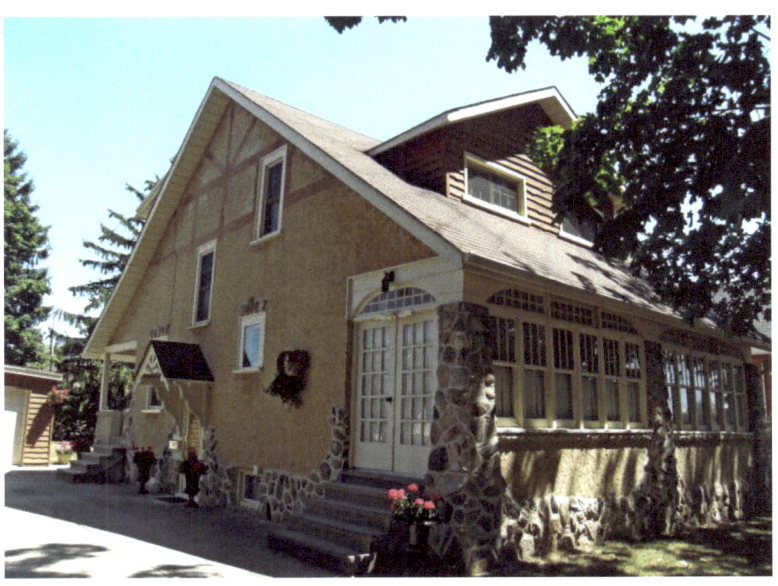

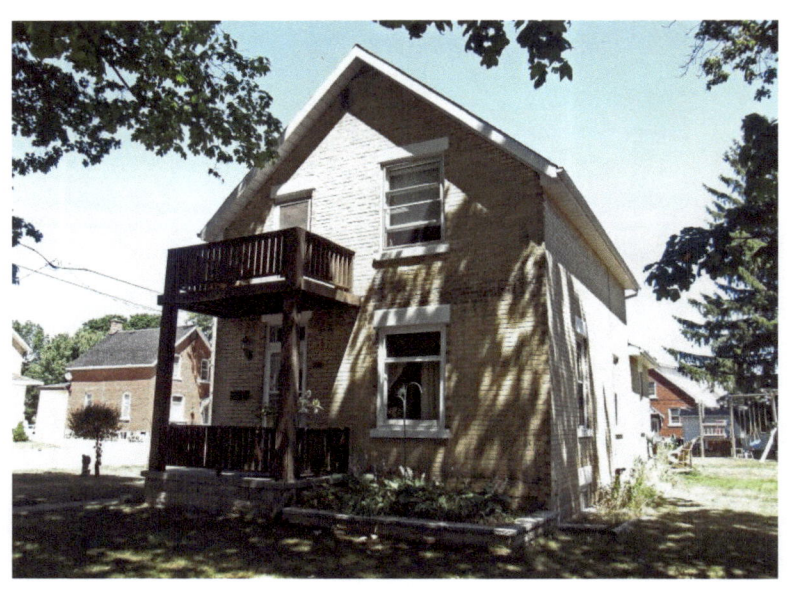

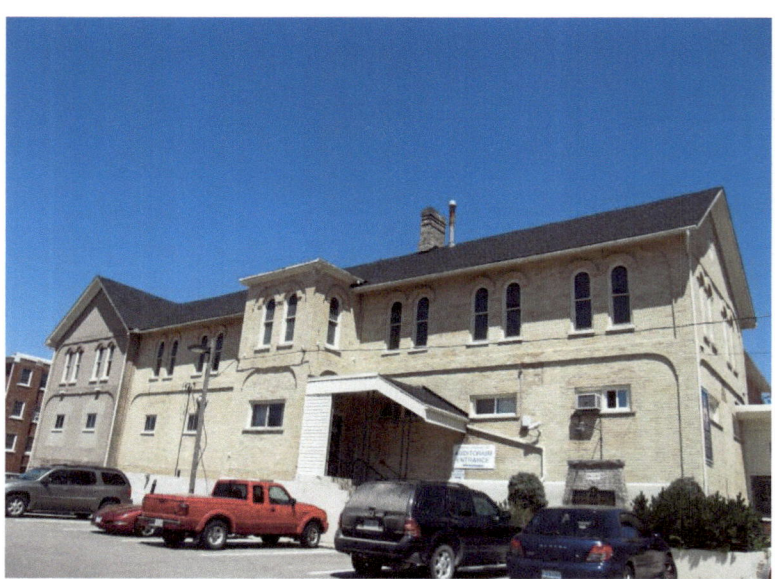

Hanover Legion Branch 130 – arched window voussoirs

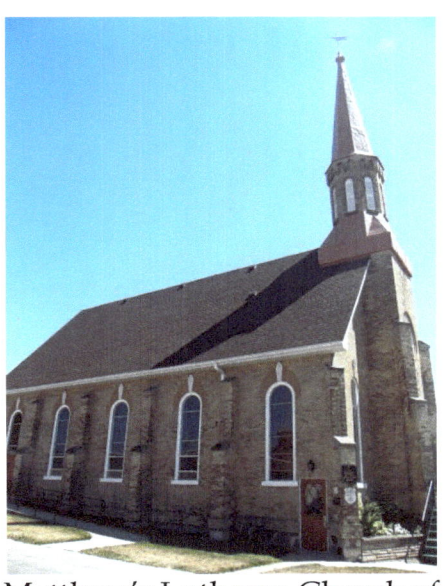

First St. Matthew's Lutheran Church of Canada
425 10th Avenue
150th anniversary – 1862-2012

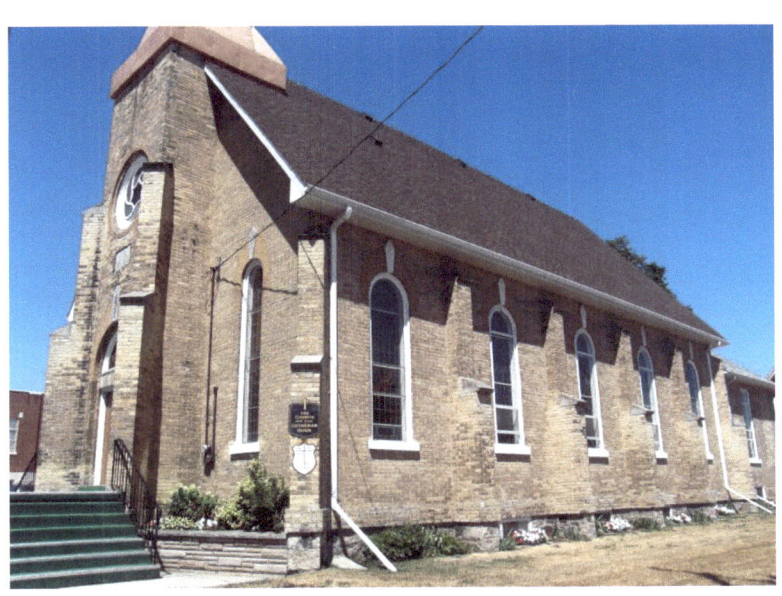

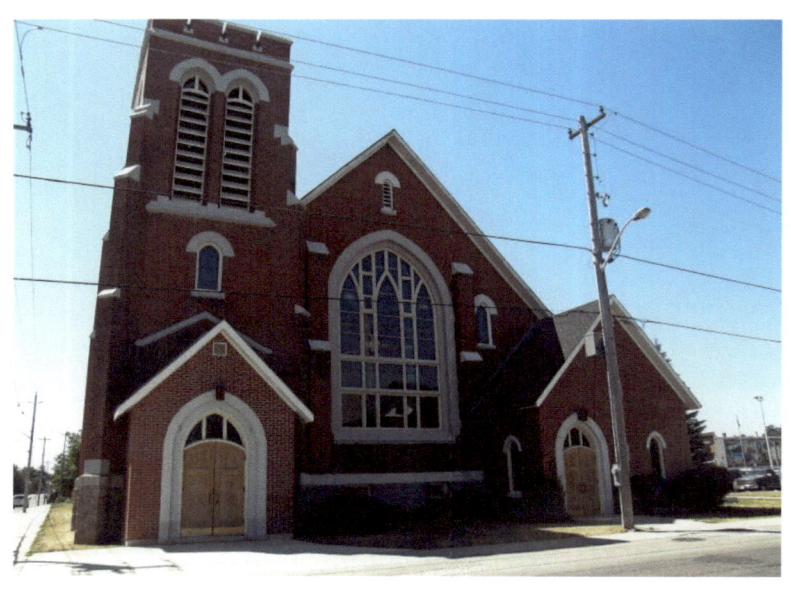

St. Matthew's Lutheran Church – A.D. 1914

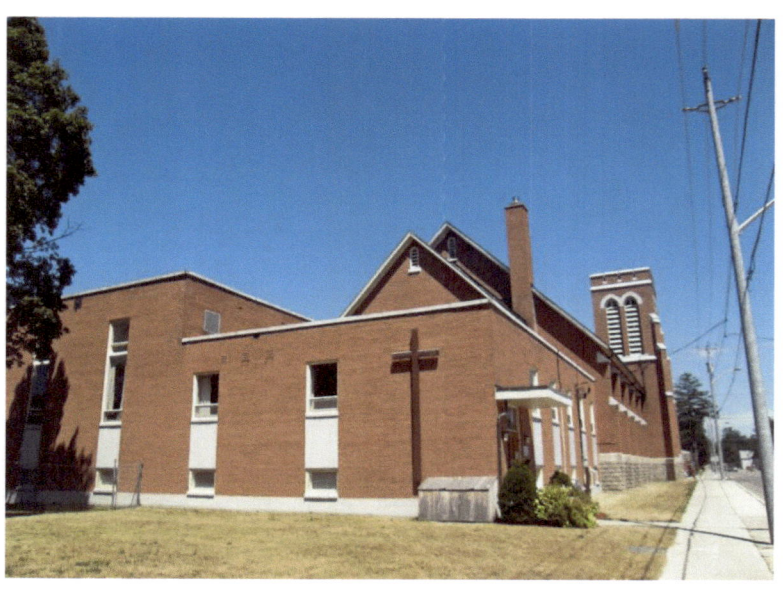

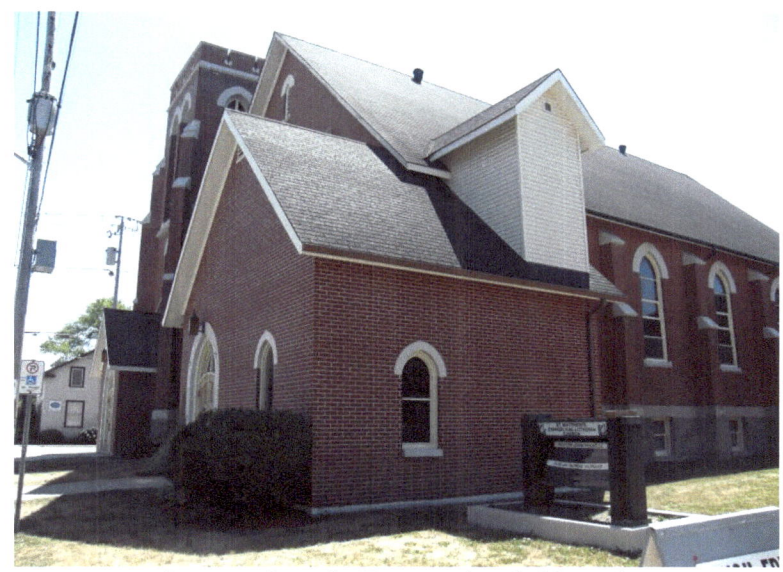

St. Matthew's Evangelical Church

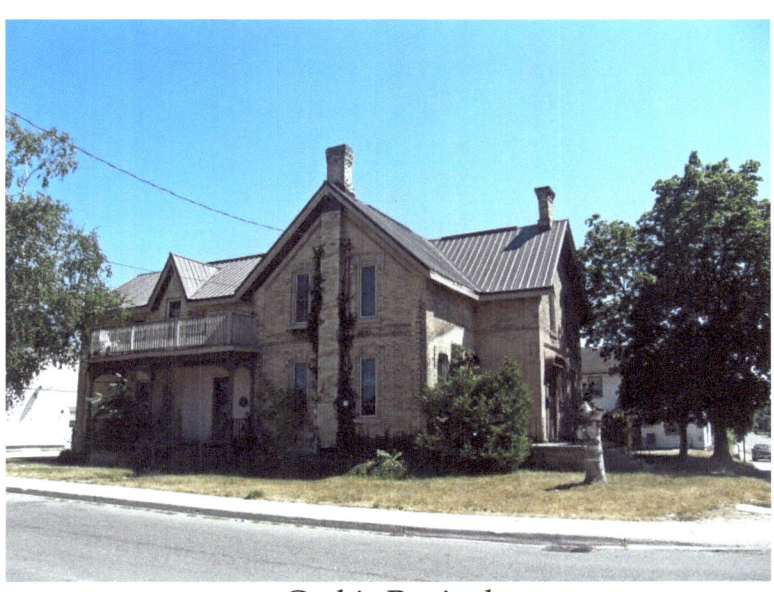

Gothic Revival

Architectural Terms

Brackets: a decorative or weight-bearing structural element which forms a right angle with one side against a wall and the other under a projecting surface such as an eave or roof.	
Buttress: a masonry structure built against or projecting from a wall which serves to support or reinforce the wall. In Canadian architecture, they are sometimes used for decoration. Example: First St. Matthew's Lutheran Church of Canada, 425 10th Avenue	
Cobblestone architecture: Refers to the use of cobblestones embedded in mortar as a method for erecting walls on houses and commercial buildings.	
Cornice: originally the wooden overhang of the roof. With the use of stone, brick, iron and steel, the cornice is any projecting shelf at the top of a ceiling or roof. They can be very decorative.	
Cornice Return: decorative element on the end of a gable. Example: Hanover Public Library	
Dentil Moulding: an even series of rectangles used as ornamental decoration in cornices.	
Dormer: (French for "sleep") a gable end window that pierces through the plane of a sloping roof surface to create usable space in the top floor or attic of a building by adding headroom. Example: 539 9th Avenue	

Fretwork: interlaced decorative design resembling a bracket	
Frontispiece: a portion of the façade of a building, usually a centred doorway that is slightly raised from the rest of the building, usually has extensive ornamentation. Frontispieces are usually Classical in design with white columned porches. Example: #512 on Page 17	
Gable: the triangular portion of a wall between the edges of a sloping roof.	
Hipped Roof: a roof where all sides slope downwards to the walls with no gables.	
Keystones and Voussoirs: a voussoir is a wedge-shaped element used in building an arch. A keystone is the central stone that locks all the stones into position, allowing the arch to bear weight. A keystone is often enlarged and embellished. Example: First St. Matthew's Lutheran Church	
Pediment: a triangular section above the horizontal structure (entablature), typically supported by columns. The inside of the triangle is called the tympanum. Example: Hanover Public Library	

Vergeboards: also called bargeboards (gingerbread) – hang from the projecting end of a roof and are often elaborately carved and ornamented. Example: Gothic Cottage (Page 16)	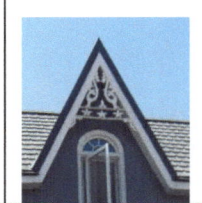

Hanover's Building Styles

Beaux Arts: Promoters of this style sought to express the classical principles on a grand and imposing scale. Many of the Beaux Arts buildings were banks, post offices, and railway stations. The Ontario Beaux Arts style is eclectic mixing elements of Classical, Renaissance and Baroque. Often the designs have a temple-like façade, pedimented porticos, balustrades, capitals in many styles Example: Hanover Public Library	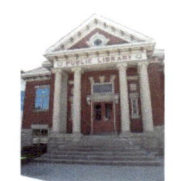
Gothic Revival, 1830-1890 – These decorative buildings have sharply-pitched gables with highly detailed vergeboards, pointed-arch window openings, and dichromatic brickwork. It is a common style in Ontario. Example:	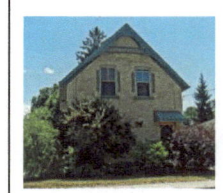
Italianate, 1850-1900 – It has wide-bracketed eaves, belvederes, wrap-around verandahs. Example: 548 8th Avenue	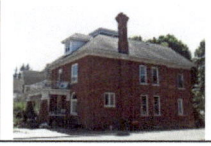